Constantin
Brancusi

$x^? \subset 7$

CONSTANTIN Brancusi

PIERRE CABANNE

TERRAIL

Cover:
The Newborn II (detail)
Before 1923
Polished bronze
17x25.5x17 cm
MNAM-Centre G. Pompidou, Paris

In memory of Peggy Guggenheim

Editorial Directors
Soline Massot and Anne Zweibaum
Editorial Assistant
Pierre Rochelois
Layout
Michel Gourtay
Translation
John Tittensor
Iconography
Nadine Gudimard
Copy editor
Catherine Roussey
Lithography
L'Exprimeur, Paris

© FINEST S.A./ÉDITIONS
PIERRE TERRAIL, PARIS 2002

Publication Number: 291
ISBN: 2-87939-242-X
Printed in Italy
June 2002

© FINEST SA / ÉDITIONS PIERRE TERRAIL, PARIS 2002
25, rue Ginoux, 75015 Paris - FRANCE

**Constantin Brancusi
in his studio c. 1927**
Photo Edward Steichen
Private collection

Contents

Bird in Space
1931/1936
Silver gelatin print
Photo Constantin Brancusi
MNAM-Centre G. Pompidou, Paris

Introduction

● Child's Head
1914/1915
Oak
16.5x25.6x18.4 cm
MNAM-Centre G. Pompidou, Paris

THE STUDIO ON IMPASSE RONSIN

Self-portrait in the studio and
tree trunk
1933/1934
Silver gelatin print
Photo Constantin Brancusi
MNAM-Centre G. Pompidou, Paris

The very antithesis of Rodin, Constantin Brancusi was one of the greatest sculptors of his century. His work, initially reminiscent of primitive and popular art, moved towards a pared-down, polished smoothness in which literal description played almost no part.

During the period 1946-1950 I was his neighbor on Impasse Ronsin, at the time a picturesquely rustic corner of Paris' 15th arrondissement, where chickens roamed free in the courtyards of studios up for demolition. At day's end you would see him standing in his doorway, as if waiting for someone. Not a tall man, he wore a long, bushy beard, a loose white tunic that reminded you of a monk's habit, and a kind of white bonnet. The lively eyes were mischievous and ironic, the look that of a crafty peasant. No tenseness about him, though, and no sign of worry. He made you think of some country sage taking the air at the end of the working day, in his case a day spent in a studio whose clutter could be glimpsed through the open door as he allowed himself a brief spell. Then he would return inside to his solitary grapplings with his creative energy. You would not see him again that night.

He ventured out only rarely and there were few callers—although, it was said, there had once been a lot of lady visitors. Apart from his painter neighbors Alexandre Istrati and his wife Natalia Dumitresco, Romanians like himself, few people saw him often; true, other artists

lived nearby, but he took no interest in them and apparently his tetchiness kept them at bay. From time to time a museum curator—generally a foreigner, with the exception of Jean Cassou—would be admitted to his lair. And yet this old man, in the course of his life in Paris, had been the friend of Modigliani and the Douanier Rousseau, Man Ray, Picabia, Léger and—especially—Erik Satie and Marcel Duchamp. Born in 1876, he was seventy-five when we met. When he came to Impasse Ronsin in 1916 he had first moved into number 8, then number 11. Gradually taking over the neighboring studios as well, he finally had five enormous, fully equipped work spaces, where he sculpted in stone and polished his steel and bronze works, endlessly refining them as part of what he called "advancing towards the divine".

In those early days he was cutting up tree trunks for the wood he wanted while Rodin, whom he admired, was living out his last years in Meudon, working his clay with powerful fingers and modeling faces and fragments of bodies. When Romanian friends introduced the young sculptor, Rodin suggested that Brancusi work with him. "Nothing grows in the shadow of tall trees," came the reply. The patriarch was suitably impressed.

At the time of our meeting, the Impasse Ronsin studios were crowded with colossal sculptures. Wooden seats and furniture Brancusi had hewn with his own hands, enormous round plaster tables and the stone fireplace, rubbed shoulders with smaller works hidden under pieces of cloth or carefully-placed dustsheets. The sculptor moved gingerly through the scrupulously ordered jumble of pieces, delicate

Previous pages

● **Brancusi's studio**
1924
Pen and Indian ink on paper
43x35.4 cm
Art Institute of Chicago

● **View of the studio**
by Brancusi
1933/1934
Silver gelatin print
Photo Constantin Brancusi
MNAM-Centre G. Pompidou, Paris

clouds of white dust rose about him. In the center of the smallest studio stood the forge, now no longer used, that had once served for heating the tools still clustered nearby.

When Brancusi accompanied me to the first of the five adjoining rooms that comprised his studio, I found myself in a deliberately self-contained world that was at once living and working space, sanctuary, laboratory, gallery and museum. A zone of silence and solitude, of whitewashed walls, peopled with ghosts as white as the old artist's beard, monk's tunic and bonnet. He cooked his meals in one area, close to a stove of monumental proportions he had made himself, worked in another—tidiness was his watchword in both—and slept in the loft, in a bed that was a sculpture in its own right.

Without a word Brancusi closed the door behind him and turned out the light. It was only later that he spoke to me.

View of the studio
1923
Silver gelatin print
Photo Constantin Brancusi
MNAM-Centre G. Pompidou, Paris

View of the studio,
Endless Columns,
Mademoiselle Pogany II
1925
Silver gelatin print
Photo Constantin Brancusi
MNAM-Centre G. Pompidou, Paris

1

1876-1907
Youth

Antin

Premiat la scóla
cele frumósa din
Bucuresti

A DUAL CULTURE: EASTERN AND POPULAR

Brancusi's spiritual life was profoundly marked by the East, and his attraction to Oriental religions and Buddhist and Zen philosophy is intimately linked to his work. A notable influence was the *Jetsun-Kahbum*, autobiographical account of the life and work of the 11th-century Tibetan mystic Milarepa—"The only book in his library of which all the pages had been cut," wrote Radu Varia[1]. "He quoted it often…" Paradoxically, the man who was to become the inventor of modern sculpture drew inspiration from the culture and spirituality of a distant, primitive past, shaping for himself a world view dating back to the dawn of Western civilization: a vision at once archaic and popular, rooted in humanity's most ancient form of expression, in the direct carving of stone and wood, in working with a material essence that is simultaneously god and mind. This very essence underlies the physical aspect of those idols and fetishes that were humanity's protectors, substitutes for the divinity, when our world was in its infancy.

Brancusi was born into an extremely simple geographical and social setting. The wine-producing area of Oltenia, where his native village of Hobitza is to be found in the canton of Pestisani, is on the west of the rich plain at the foot of the southern Carpathians—whence the nickname "the Carpathian shepherd" sometimes applied to him—and well away from the big cities. The way of life he described as "beautiful and

harmonious" had remained unchanged for centuries, rooted in patri-archal traditions that left an unequivocal mark on him during his teenage years.

His family was well off. Nicolae, his father, was the administrator of the lands belonging to the Tismana Monastery to the west of Tirgu-Jiu, a town later to become indissociable from the sculptor's life and work.

It is said that Brancusi had a difficult childhood, his smallness of stature making him the butt of his brothers' jokes. After primary school he worked for a dyer in Tirgu-Jiu, then spent time in Pestisani and Craiova, apparently earning a living from a variety of "odd jobs". He was of an unstable temperament, writing that at one point he had "roamed the country for six years, completely out of touch with his family". At eighteen, having attracted widespread admiration with a violin he had made, he entered the School of Arts and Crafts in Craiova, where his woodworking skills became highly respected.

Yet the urge to see the world continued to gnaw at him and in the summer of 1897 he took ship for Vienna, the first step towards the West. There he became apprenticed to Herr Roth, who later provided him with a "certificate of proficiency".

On returning to Craiova, he began making wooden furniture. He was chronically dissatisfied with his work, but it was good enough to earn him a place in the School of Fine Art in Bucharest, where he studied sculpture under recognized masters such as Ion Georgescu, showed impressive ability and graduated in 1902. He then decided to sign over his part of the family inheritance—land he knew he would never be able to farm—to his brothers, and to pay for further studies by once again doing odd jobs around Craiova. At the same time he joined a chorale and learnt Gregorian chant, being deeply moving by its richness and sonority.

Brancusi's first commission, for the Central Military Hospital in Bucharest, was a bust of Surgeon-General Carol Davila, whom he had already portrayed in a bas-relief. In full uniform, the general is shown sporting superb sidewhiskers and a plumed kepi. Brancusi brought a similarly academic spirit to his bust of Ion Georgescu-Gorjan, a well-known Craiova personality, serious of mien and impressively mustached[2].

Then in May 1904, he left for Paris.

Romanian Peasant
(Study of a figure
in traditional costume)
Undated
Pencil and charcoal
Muzeul National de Arta al Romanici, Bucharest

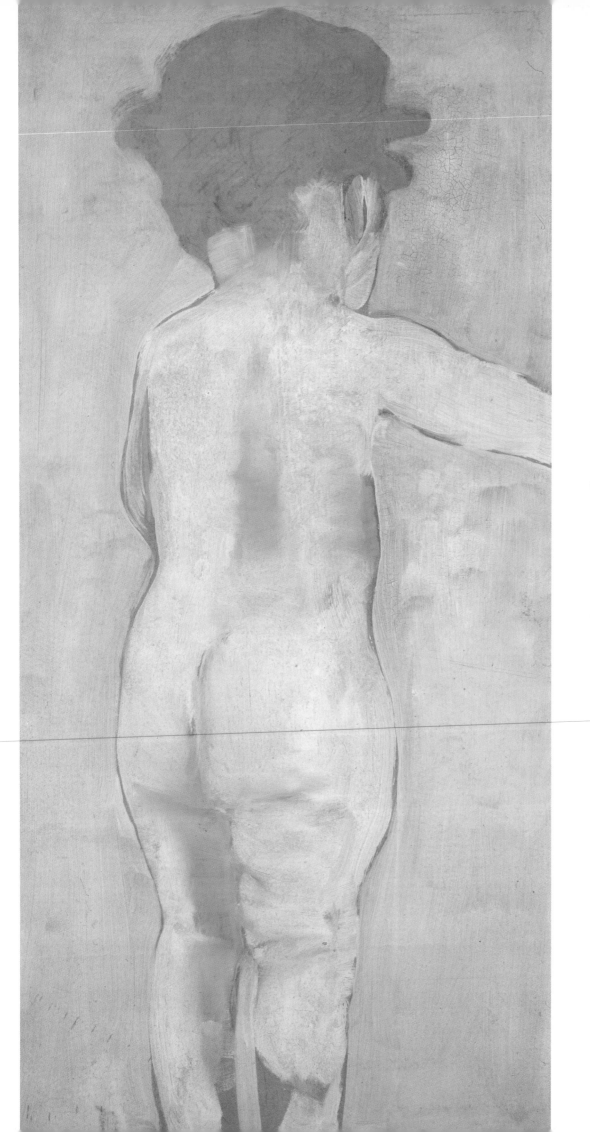

The First Step

c. 1912

Oil on cardboard

60.8x28.9 cm

Art Institute of Chicago

Portrait of a woman (profile)

c. 1912

Oil on paper

53.5x41.4 cm

Collection Mrs John M. Shoenberg

Yet the young artist's true, essential inspiration lay in the woodworking techniques of which so many illustrations are still to be found in Romania's churches and dwelling: balcony posts, struts, cabled columns, stacked rhomboids and sculpted, ornamented household objects. Motifs such as the sun, tracery, spirals, rope moldings and circles inset with crosses were abundant in ceramics and embroidery. Brancusi was constantly exposed to this formal repertoire—often the work of his fellow craftsmen in Craiova. The town museum, too, contained stimulating examples of sculpted furniture, ceramics, embroidery and tapestries decorated with human figures and symbolic shapes.

The young Brancusi found the Village Museum in Bucharest even more fascinating, not only for its extraordinary setting between Lake Herastrau and the Kisseleff causeway, where a long, shady avenue leads the visitor to the entrance, but also because its nine hectares and more were home to some three hundred buildings taken from all over the country. His family's house in Hobitza would not have been out of place there. A stunning summary of Romanian popular architecture and art, the museum also includes reconstructed interiors, workshops specializing in wrought iron, ceramics and embroidery, and two painted and decorated churches: one dating from 1727 brought from Maramures, a woodworking region par excellence, and the other, also 18th-century, from Moldavia.

Traditional Romanian houses [details]

A GRAVELY SERENE LITURGY

Direct carving of stone and wood harks back to primitive and popular art forms, giving expression, in its sheer energy, concentration of thought, and strength and sureness of hand, to the act of taking possession of the material. Leaving the sculptor no possibility of turning back or correcting a mistake, and founded, to quote Gaston Bachelard, on "the discovery of form via the of the formless", the process has always had a religious character. As manifestations of nature, stone and wood embody something of its mysterious power; they are spiritualized by their origins and the sculptor not only taps into their deepest energy but also their magical force. The most ancient stone and wooden idols are imbued with this potency, a life of their own; they are not works of art, but sacred objects expressing the generative impetus of their maker. The material is spirit, containing and releasing the spirit.

The presence of Brancusi's sculptures transformed his studios into a temple, a sacred space, a domain set aside for the enactment of a grave, serene liturgy to whose rites no other sculptor had access. In contemporary sculpture to which he brought a new language, this solitary, secretive man, fascinated by the telluric forces of our earliest beginnings, appears as a demiurge, the prophet of the art that was to come.

FIRST MAJOR WORK: *THE PRAYER*

In April 1907 Brancusi was agreeably surprised to receive his first significant commission, a monument in the Dumbrava cemetery at Buzau, a large industrial town to the north-east of Bucharest. The widow of a local notable, Petre Stanescu, wished to honor her husband's memory; but why choose Brancusi, an unknown living in faraway Paris? True, the young sculptor had achieved a certain success in the Paris Salons and had the backing of painter Stefan Popescu, whose bust he had exhibited at the Salon d'Automne in 1906 and at the Tinerimea Artistica in Bucharest a year later. But does this explain his being singled out in a country where grandiloquent funerary sculpture was very much a living form and its masters much sought after?

The Prayer
1907, erected in the Dumbrava
cemetery, Buzau, in 1914
on the tomb of Petre Stanescu
Patinated bronze
Muzeul National de Arta al Romanici, Bucharest

The Prayer
1907
Bronze
112x33.5x121.5 cm
Muzeul National de Arta al Romanici, Bucharest

Doubtless the insistence of Doctor Garota, professor of anatomy at the School of Arts and Crafts in Bucharest and formerly Brancusi's teacher, also worked in his favor. But would it be entirely mistaken to see here another example of the links between those shadowy guilds and their initiates?

The monument was certainly intended to be imposing. The contract drawn up between Brancusi and Ms. Stanescu in Paris on 18 April 1907 —this would suggest that she actually visited the artist at that time— stipulates a stone pedestal over 2 meters high, a bust of the deceased and "an allegorical figure representing a woman weeping beside the pedestal". The artist was to be paid in monthly installments and was responsible for the transport of the finished work from Paris to Buzau. *The Prayer*, now housed in the Fine Arts Museum in Bucharest[6], is a work of moving simplicity. Leaning forward with its hands joined and ovoid head slightly bent, free of all unnecessary detail, the naked figure kneels on its marble base as the bust of Petre Stanescu, executed from photographs, looks down from the height of its stele. Cast in bronze and first shown at the Salon des Indépendants in 1910, *The Prayer* was erected in Buzau in 1914, being met there with a certain

● **The Newborn**
c. 1930
Silver gelatin print
Photo Constantin
Brancusi
MNAM-Centre G. Pompidou, Paris

● **The Newborn II**
Before 1923
Plaster
17.5x25.2x17.2 cm
MNAM-Centre G. Pompidou, Paris

bafflement. Fortunately the distance between Brancusi and Bucharest art circles spared him the barbs of the local patriotic and funerary sculpture specialists.

A month after the commission for the Buzau gravestone, the young sculptor was officially informed in a letter from the Romanian Ministry of Education that his plaster *Bust of a Boy*, exhibited at the Tinerimea Artistica in Bucharest, had been bought by the Fine Arts Museum, where it can still be seen today. The sadness of the boy's expression, so eloquently captured in the photo taken by Brancusi himself, is most affecting. As for *The Newborn* of the same period, the skull is a smooth ovoid, a shape that was to become a recurrent feature of his oeuvre: Brancusi identified it with the egg, its hard, hermetic container and soft interior symbolizing the fertility principle and the emergence of life. It was as if he knew intuitively that he was to beget a new form of sculpture.

● **Sleeping Child**
1908(?)
White marble
11x16.5x14.5 cm
MNAM-Centre G. Pompidou, Paris

The Newborn II ●
Before 1923
Polished bronze.
Four-part base: polished bronze, white marble, oak and stone
Total height: 86 cm
MNAM-Centre G. Pompidou, Paris

The Kiss

1909
Stone
28x26x21.5 cm

Montparnasse Cemetery, Paris

Medallion of the Kiss

c. 1909
Silver gelatin print

Photo Constantin Brancusi

MNAM-Centre G. Pompidou, Paris

The Kiss
1910
Photo highlighted with
white gouache
Photo Constantin Brancusi
Whereabouts unknown

**Column of the Kiss
in the studio**
c. 1916/1917
Photo Constantin Brancusi
MNAM-Centre G. Pompidou, Paris

2

1908-1912
Maturation

INTENSE EXPERIMENTATION

Portrait of Brancusi
c. 1930

In Paris' Montparnasse cemetery a variant in stone of *The Kiss* — the intertwined bodies crouch face to face, knee to knee, in 89 centimeters of utter vertical symmetry—was set on a stele overlooking the grave of Tania Rachevskaia[10], a young Russian anarchist who had committed suicide for love. Her family did not care at all for this odd monument and suggested modifications, but Brancusi would not acquiesce. In his view only the symbol of love could pay adequate tribute to such a death. The Montparnasse *Kiss* was the first Brancusi monument to be erected in Paris; it remains the only one.

Brancusi was living at the time on Rue du Montparnasse, not far from the Rue d'Odessa studio where he had installed a forge and anvil. Among his neighbors was Steichen, the American photographer, who offered advice and took pictures of his work. Brancusi exhibited at the Salon d'Automne, created portraits that have since been lost and made his first venture into direct carving of marble with *Sleep*[11]. This work's classicism is in sharp contrast with *Head*[12], whose manner owes much to the Romanesque, Brancusi's preferred medieval period. *Sleep* belonged to Guillaume Apollinaire, of whom the least that can be said is that he took no great interest in its creator.

Throughout this experimental period Brancusi, certain of his technical mastery and determined to maintain his pared-down style, carefully kept his distance from the too-direct influences that his peasant

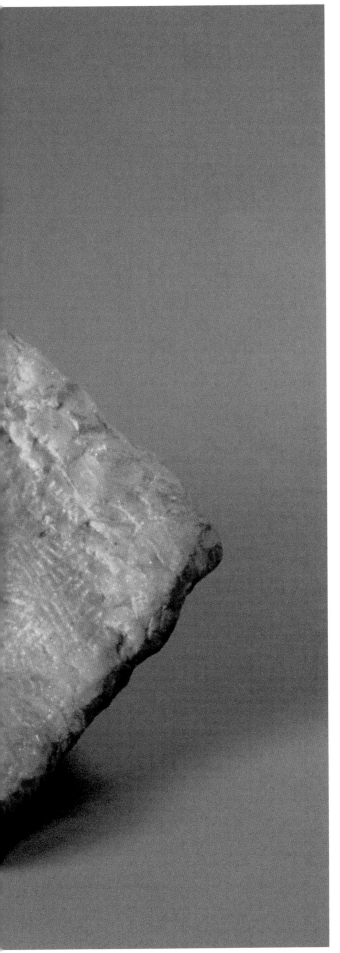

shrewdness had taught him to distrust. In both *The Kiss* and *The Prayer* he sought symbolic expression of two forms of love, both informed by the notion of death that spiritualizes and perpetuates the union of two human beings. While not directly inspired by primitivism, he adopted its simplicity, spirituality and earthiness. His love of the archaic art of Greece, the Greco-Buddhist sculpture of the Gandhara school and early medieval sculpture can be explained by the fact that all three were periods of new beginnings.

Yet he did not frequent museums and proud monuments: what affected him most was the spirit of the work—direct contact with it— rather than the work itself. The only thing he really seized on at this time, and solely in order to take the opposite direction, was Rodin's "beefcake" approach.

Carving and burnishing a block of soapstone, in 1908 he created *Wisdom of the Earth*. Seated with knees drawn up and arms folded across her chest, this naked adolescent girl has sightless eyes in a rounded face with barely suggested features, and the same rippling, back-drawn hair as *Head of a Girl*. Disconcertingly, she does not seem to belong to her chunky body, which renders the work as a whole even more enigmatic.

What, then, is her inner mystery? There have been attempts to pin down her genesis, make her yield up her secret, but their labored bathos only complicates the question. Radu Varia, for example, wrote that in *Wisdom of the Earth* Brancusi "draws his vision...from the abyssal irrationality of his own immemorial quickening...from beyond the furthest reaches of his heritage and his lineage."

"Brancusi's genius," Mircea Eliade[13] stated, "lies in knowing where to seek the true 'source' of the forms he felt himself capable of creating."

Following pages:

Danaide
c. 1908/1909
Stone
33x26x24 cm
Muzeul National de Arta al Romanici, Bucharest

Head of a Bodhisattva
6/7th century
Clay, 25x21x21 cm
MNAA-Guimet, Paris

Sleep
1908
Marble
26x43.5x32.3 cm
Muzeul National de Arta
al Romanici, Bucharest

Sleeping Muse
1910
Polished bronze
16x25x18 cm
MNAM-Centre G. Pompidou, Paris

Douanier Rousseau
Self-portrait
by Lamplight
1902/1903
Oil on canvas
23x19 cm
Musée Picasso, Paris

Sleeping Muse III (study)
1917/1918 (?)
Marble
18.5x29.5
Private collection

the series of faces and busts of Renée Frachon. Cast in five slightly different examples, one of which, in gilded bronze, was offered by the sitter to the Musée National d'Art Moderne in Paris, this work was also the first in a succession of ovoids whose ultimate refinement Brancusi would seek for a quarter of a century: a shape verging on cosmic infinity, achieved, as Ezra Pound would put it, "by the highest possible consciousness of a formal perfection as pared down as the philosophical demands of a Paradiso could make it…"

On 2 September 1910, the Douanier Rousseau died in the Necker Hospital in Paris. We know little of his relationship with Brancusi beyond the fact that the sculptor enjoyed attending his musical evenings and was present at the famous party given by Apollinaire and Picasso at the Bateau-Lavoir in 1908. This latter was a kind of gigantic practical joke that turned into a tumultuous tribute to the old man and left him in a state of dazed delight.

Brancusi related having watched Rousseau paint *The Muse and the Poet*, scrupulously taking Apollinaire's measurements and transferring them to the canvas while two disciples played violins under his supervision. "He was open, honest and honorable," he commented, "not at all naive, but with a kind of candor about him…" Rousseau had come to see him in his studio, telling him, "I can see what you're after, you want to turn the ancient into the modern[19]."

After the Douanier's death, Brancusi was asked by some of his friends to create a monument to him, but the project came to nothing. However, he and the painter Oriz de Zarate engraved a poem by Apollinaire on his gravestone in the cemetery at Bagneux, reproducing the poet's handwriting[20].

LIFE IN MONTPARNASSE, 1910-1920

On 15 May 1912, Brancusi rented a second studio on the opposite side of Rue du Montparnasse, at number 47. In a watercolor dating from 1915 he portrays himself in the courtyard, energetically striking an anvil with a hammer under the watchful eye of a spectator who could be either male or female.

Then little more than a country town, Montparnasse was taking over from Montmartre as the artist's quarter. In October 1912 Picasso moved to Boulevard Raspail, then Rue Schoelcher, overlooking the cemetery. A year later the pro-Cubist avant-garde review *Les Soirées de Paris* followed him there, to number 278. At the Closerie des Lilas, opposite the famous Bal Bullier, Apollinaire, Salmon and Cendrars rubbed shoulders with the last cohort of symbolist poets. While never a "Monparnassian", Brancusi was nonetheless a local character, with his thick, dark beard, his *căciulă*—the curious bonnet worn by Romanian peasants—and his long tunic. He was often to be seen in the company of a still little-known musician, a strange figure who used to walk all the way

Marevna (Marie Vorobleff)
Homage to the Artists of Montparnasse
Undated
Oil on canvas
160x305 cm
Private collection, Paris

Chocolate Grinder No. 1

1913

Oil on canvas

31.5x23 cm

Philadelphia Museum of Art

Steamship propeller

Brancusi, Tristan Tzara
and Mina Loy in the studio
1921/1922.

from Arcueil: Erik Satie, whose weirdness and humor were much to Brancusi's taste, as his "Day in the Life of a Musician", written in 1912, makes clear.

In the cafés the two would run into Modigliani, the Russians—Chagall, Soutine, Zadkine—from La Ruche ("The Beehive", a tumbledown artists' residence in the 14th arrondissement), the first foreign members of the School of Paris, and models not averse to brief encounters.

In 1912 Léger, who had a studio on Avenue du Maine, joined Brancusi and mutual friend Marcel Duchamp for a visit to the Paris Air Show. "Now that's what I call a sculpture!" Brancusi suddenly exclaimed, coming to a dead halt in front of a propeller. "From now on sculpture must be nothing less than that!" Thirty years later he would still bring up this meeting with "perfect form". According to Léger, Duchamp reacted in exactly the same way: "It's all over for painting. Who could better that propeller? Tell me, can you do that?"

At the Salon des Indépendants in 1912 Brancusi exhibited *Prometheus*[24], an ovoid on a base that complemented *Sleeping Muse*, also on show, and *The Kiss*. "In the sculpture section," Apollinaire reported laconically in the *Intransigeant* for 29 March, "three names are worth a mention: Brancusi, Centore and Archipenko." Perhaps it was remorse that lay behind his reference on April 5 to "Brancusi, a sensitive, highly personal sculptor whose pieces show great delicacy", but he was still hardly committing himself. The same offhandedness marked his "interesting pieces by Brancusi and Agéro…" in the *Montjoie* of 29 March 1913, when Brancusi exhibited his polished bronze *Maiastra*.

Apollinaire only made matters worse in a note appended to his *Peintres Cubistes: Méditations Esthétiques* of 1913: "Among the sculptors trying to edge into the Cubist school, we should mention, apart from Mr Duchamp-Villon, Messrs Auguste Agéro, Archipenko and Brancusi (*sic*)…"

Brancusi would doubtless have been happier with Roger Allard's evaluation in the *Revue de France et des Pays Français* of April 1912: "There is a delightful purity of style about Brancusi's *Sleeping Muse*…but for sheer expressive force the work is outstripped by *Prometheus* and above all *The Kiss*, by the tranquil potency of its architecture."

Amadeo Modigliani
Portrait of
Jacques Lipchitz
c. 1917
Pencil
Marlborough Fine Art Ltd.

Erik Satie

Following page:
Prometheus
1911
Marble
13.8x17.8x13.7 cm
Philadelphia Museum of Art

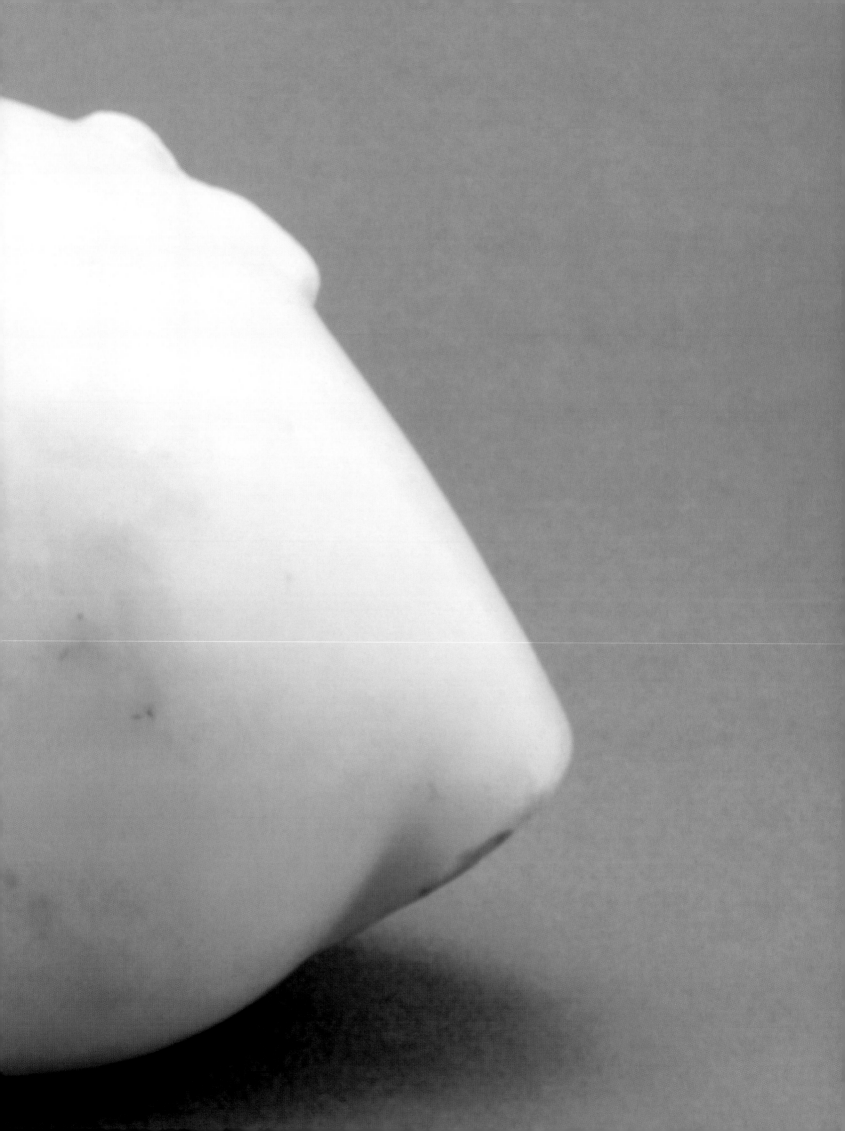

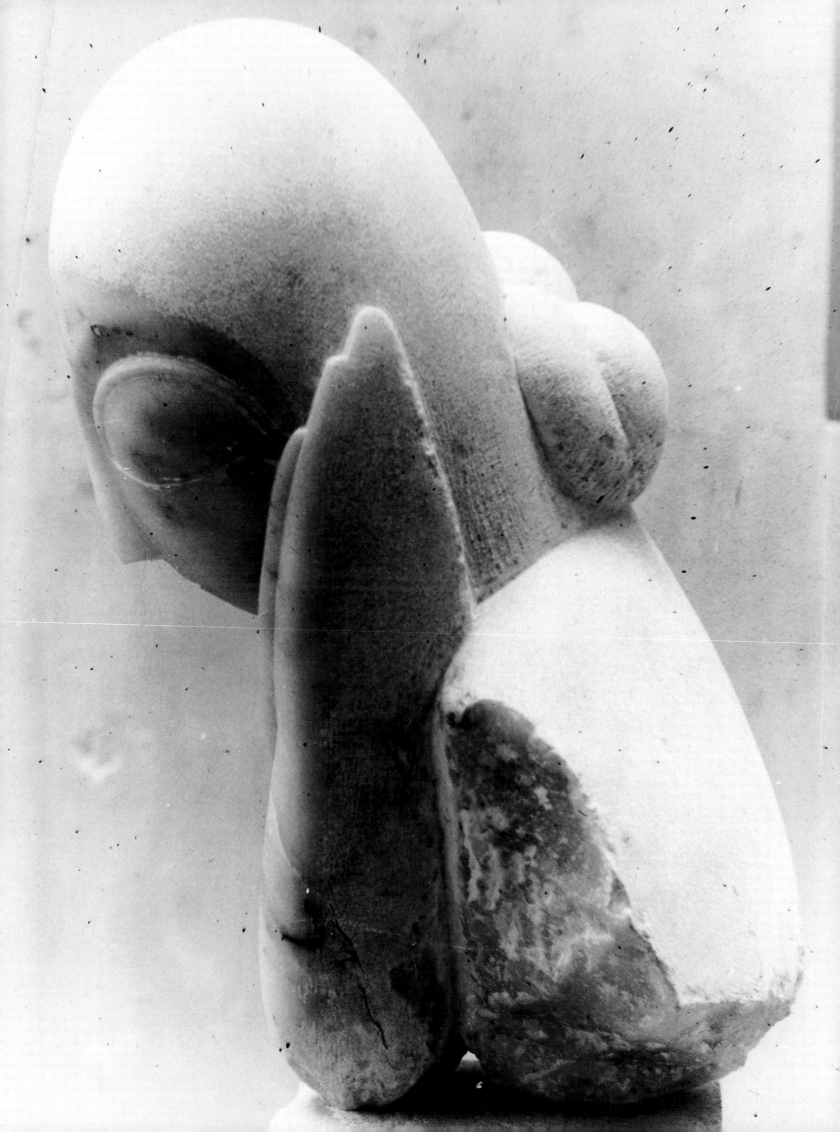

Previous pages:

● **Danaide**
Before 1922
27.5x16x19.6 cm
MNAM-Centre G. Pompidou, Paris

● **Mademoiselle Pogany I**
1920
Silver gelatin print
Photo Constantin Brancusi
MNAM-Centre G. Pompidou, Paris

MADEMOISELLE POGANY

Study for
Mademoiselle Pogany ●
1912
Pencil on paper
54.6x41.9 cm
Philadelphia Museum of Art

The studio: in the center,
● **Mademoiselle Pogany II**
Silver gelatin print
Photo Constantin Brancusi
MNAM-Centre G. Pompidou, Paris

In the same year, 1912, work began on the portrait of Margit Pogany. Brancusi had met the young painter, daughter of a well known Hungarian lawyer of Romanian descent, in Montparnasse in 1910, when she was exhibiting at the Salon d'Automne. They immediately became friends and saw each other often. On visiting his studio, she noticed that his busts were "nothing but eyes". From December 1910, when he asked her to sit for him, through January 1911, when she left Paris for Lausanne, they were lovers, as her letters to him make clear: "I've been thinking of you so much, and of how kind and tender you've been with me...I should like to give you all the joy that you give me." Brancusi kept these letters, two of which now belong to MOMA in New York. She also sent him a specially commissioned French translation of Goethe's *Prometheus*.

Having destroyed all the preliminary versions produced during the two months she had sat for him, Brancusi found himself forced to finish the bust without a model: for reasons that remain unknown, Margit Pogany never returned. However, they continued to exchange letters, the young woman declaring her impatience to see the work, her readiness to pay the casting costs—and her hope of selling the bust "for the highest possible price", a notion that left the sculptor at something of a loss.

In February 1913, the plaster version of *Mademoiselle Pogany*, since lost, was dispatched to the famous Armory Show in New York. Recommended by Duchamp, Brancusi had been invited to participate by the critic and painter Walter Pach, himself being asked to investigate the Paris scene by the Association of American Painters and

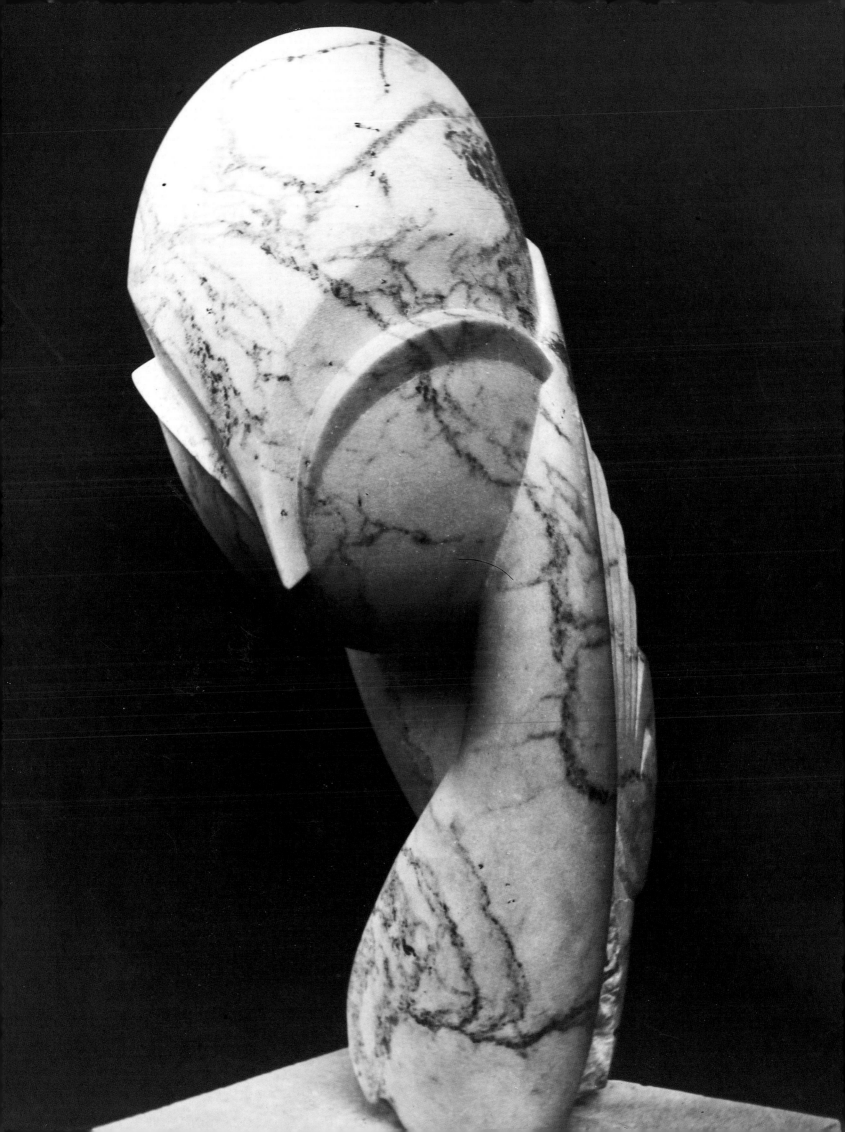

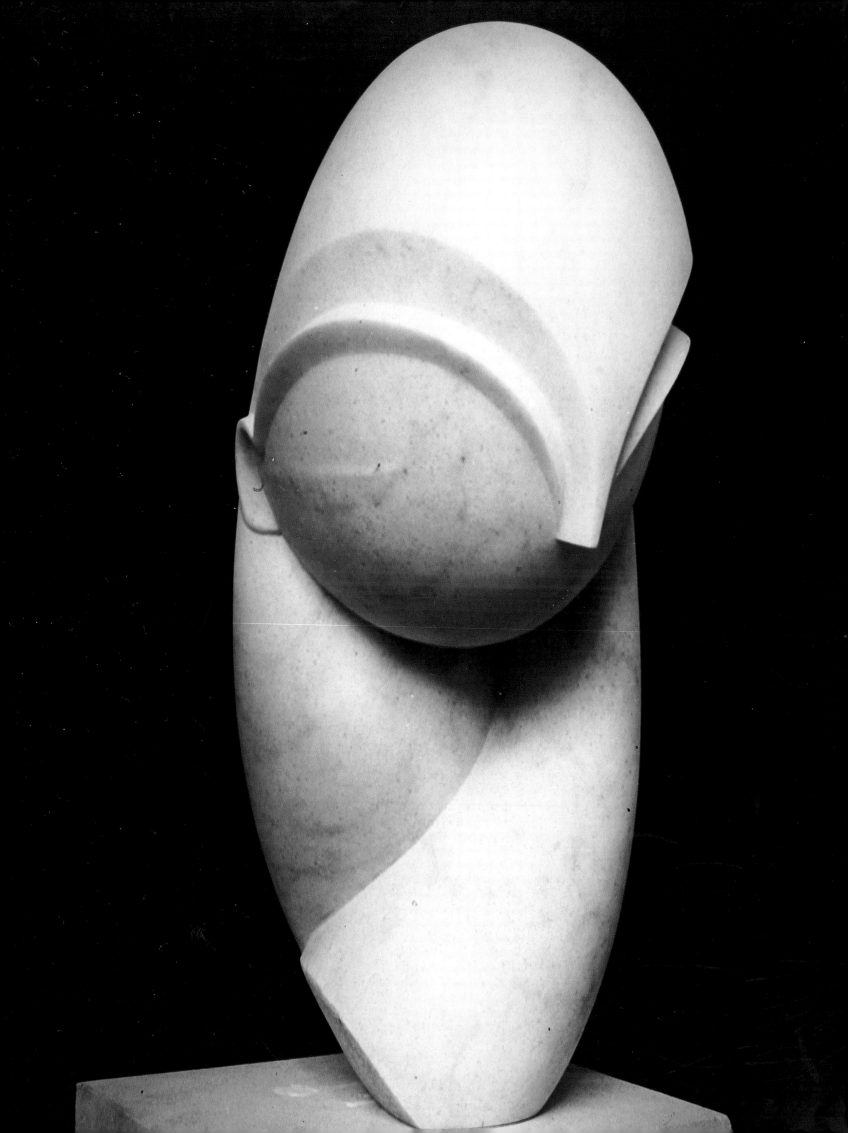

Sculptors. When Pach and the Association's president, Arthur B. Davies, came to look at the studio, they were accompanied by Walt Kuhn, a mediocre painter: "That's the kind of guy I'm doing this show for," remarked Brancusi.

At the Armory Show the plaster of *Mademoiselle Pogany* appeared on a kind of large base, together with the other works Brancusi had sent: *The Muse* and *Sleeping Muse*, both in marble, *The Kiss* in stone and a 1912 marble *Torso of a Girl*, listed in the catalogue supplement. Duchamp's *Nude Descending a Staircase* and Picabia's *Dance at the Fountain* provoked an enormous scandal and when the show moved to Chicago a group of students, urged on by their teachers, burnt effigies of Matisse, Picasso, Walter Pach—and Brancusi.

On 21 February 1913, just after the opening of the exhibition, Walter Pach recounted to Brancusi the reception his bust had been given: "You've had an enormous success at the show, people love your work and you're all over the papers." However, the reactions were not all favorable, with visitors pitilessly scoffing at *Sleeping Muse* and *Mademoiselle Pogany* and an anonymous bit of doggerel heaping derision on *The Kiss*. As Walter Pach commented, "Here is a new man for this country, one whose output seems too strange for most people to understand…"

Nonetheless, after the Armory Show, several rich Americans—Lizzie Bliss and Mary B. Sullivan, Arthur B. Davies and the lawyer John Quinn—began collecting Paris artists, with Gertrude and Leo Stein acting as intermediaries. Visiting studios was part of a collector's education and Brancusi's was on the list.

When the bust of Margit Pogany had been cast in bronze, he sent it to her in Bucharest. "I'm glad you sent me the bronze," she wrote back, "I prefer it to the marble. The color you've put into it really brings out its feral, archaic side, yet at the same time, makes it more natural[26]…"

Previous pages:

Mademoiselle Pogany II
1919
Silver gelatin negative on glass plate
Photo Constantin Brancusi
MNAM-Centre G. Pompidou, Paris

Mademoiselle Pogany III
1931
Silver gelatin negative on glass plate
Photo Constantin Brancusi
MNAM-Centre G. Pompidou, Paris

Mademoiselle Pogany III
1933
44.5x19x27 cm
Bronze, two-part base: stone and oak
Height: 124 cm
MNAM-Centre G. Pompidou, Paris

Mademoiselle Pogany I
1912/1913
Plaster
45.5x23.4x23.4 cm
MNAM-Centre G. Pompidou, Paris

3

1913-1918
First successes

THE FIRST SOLO EXHIBITION
AND THE BEGINNINGS OF A REPUTATION

In the studio
1923
Photo Constantin Brancusi
MNAM-Centre G. Pompidou, Paris

I n July 1913 Brancusi exhibited several works at the sixth Allied Artists salon in London, and again at the Doré gallery in October. "As far as sculpture goes," wrote the famous critic Roger Fry, "the works of Brancusi were the most remarkable in the show."

Brancusi took advantage of the Allied Artists exhibition to go to London and visit the British Museum, where he spent hours in the African art collection. He also visited the sculptor Jacob Epstein, who had called on him the year before.Highly intrigued both by Epstein's collection of tribal art and his work—in 1911 he had been commissioned to create Oscar Wilde's tombstone, considered outrageous when erected at Paris' Père Lachaise cemetery—he was to feel their influence on his return to Paris. During his stay in France Epstein had also met Rodin, Picasso, Modigliani, Derain and the future art dealer Paul Guillaume, who had shown him his collection of African art.

In 1913 and 1914, Brancusi took part in the Tinerimea Artistica in Bucharest. He was invited to show in Prague in February 1914 by French art critic Alexandre Mercereau, his work appearing alongside that of Duchamp-Villon, Archipenko and various Czech artists.

At the same time as his plaster *Mademoiselle Pogany*[27] was on display at the Armory Show, a version in white marble was being exhibited at the Sculptors' Gallery in New York. The latter was still in New York the following year, at Photo-Secession, run by Alfred Stieglitz, one of

modern art's main sponsors in the United States. Walter Pach had expressed misgivings about the venue, but the exposition was a great success in terms of recognition and sales: in spite of prices ranging from 2,000 to 5,000 francs, only two pieces went unsold. This was Brancusi's first solo exhibition, at age 38 and in a country where he was now finding his most enthusiastic admirers. In France he still passed unnoticed, no critics visited his studio and press reports on the salons where he exhibited made no mention of his novelty and originality. Even the strangeness of his work went unremarked. It would take a "scandal" some years later, in 1920, to get his name and work into the news.

Child's Head

Head of The First Step

1917

Plaster

16.9x26x19 cm

MNAM-Centre G. Pompidou, Paris

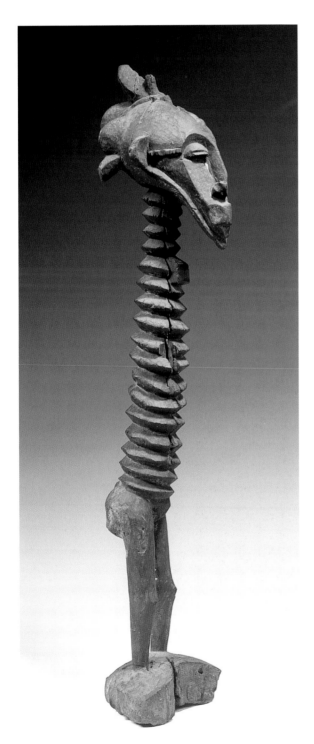

Little French Girl

or Little Girl

or The First Step III

1914/1918(?)

Oak

123.5x23.8x23.5 cm

The Solomon R. Guggenheim Museum, New York

Senufo Mask

Early 20th century

Red wood with

brownish patina

76.2x19x19 cm

Musée National,
Abidjan, Ivory Coast

Jacques Lipchitz
Sailor Playing a Guitar
1914/1915
Gilded bronze
77.5x29x24.5 cm
MNAM-Centre G. Pompidou, Paris

Jacques Lipchitz
Figure
1926/1930
Painted plaster
220x95x75 cm
MNAM-Centre G. Pompidou, Paris

The First Cry
1917
Cement
18.5x25.5x17 cm
Two-part wood base
Total height: 102,6 cm
Private collection

THE FIRST STEP: AN AMBIGUOUS RETURN TO AFRICA

In the same year as *Mademoiselle Pogany*, or perhaps a little before, Brancusi produced a strange wooden figure that he exhibited at Photo-Secession but then destroyed, except for the head, after photographing it on his return. *The First Step* presents a curiously disjointed child trotting forward. We know that even if African art was a major concern for Brancusi—he had been struck by the statuettes and fetishes seen in museums and the houses of Dr Alexandre and other friends—he distrusted its influence. After *The Kiss* and *Maiastra*, he was drawn to new forms, perhaps as a consequence of his visit to the British Museum in July 1913 and his meeting with Epstein. It can be conjectured that they visited Modigliani together in Paris and saw his oblong, simplified heads. Without a doubt, the direction Brancusi now took had a range of sources, themselves born of the equally numerous suppositions, comparisons and transpositions Picasso, Matisse and Derain had already worked through in respect of primitivism.

Sidney Geist[28] has described *The First Step* as "Brancusi's first truly independent and original work…" Brancusi himself gave full credit to the revelatory role played by tribal art and its highly individual character in the development of contemporary art, but always resisted the idea of its influence on himself. Romanian art historians flatly reject any such influence. Indeed, the primary reason for Brancusi's interest in African sculpture would seem to be its use of wood, the characteristic

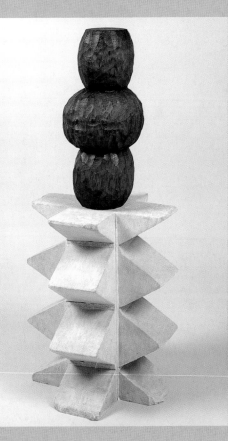

● **Base**

1927

Partially stained oak

80x25x39 cm

MNAM-Centre G. Pompidou, Paris

● **Exotic Plant**

1923/1924

Wood and stone

92.5x38x38 cm

MNAM-Centre G. Pompidou, Paris

● **Base**

c. 1925

Plaster and oak

MNAM-Centre G. Pompidou, Paris

Study for
Mrs Eugene Meyer, Jr
1916/1933
Walnut
84x19x23 cm
Three-part base: stone
and walnut
MNAM-Centre G. Pompidou, Paris

View of Brancusi's studio
c. 1930/1933
Photo Constantin Brancusi
MNAM-Centre G. Pompidou, Paris

THE FIRST *ENDLESS COLUMN*

Little French Girl begins like *The First Step*, only to achieve a totally different configuration and spirit. Set on a base, the piece comprises a long, tapering vertical section, ringed with grooves, which is both the torso and neck of a figure perched on a pair of spindly legs. The head is a kind of helmet whose inverted appearance is repeated in the girl's bell-shaped skirt. The Senufo model pointed out by William Rubin and commented upon by Sidney Geist is clearly in evidence and the Bambara statuette behind *The First Step* no less so. But here there is a touch of humor as well.

Brancusi's "Negro" period can be dated to 1913-20 and gave him the opportunity to try several different kinds of wood: apart from *The First Step* and *Little French Girl*, it includes the *Portrait of Madame L. R.* (1914-17), the *Portrait of Mrs Eugene Meyer* (1916), *Caryatid* (old oak, 1916), *The Prodigal Son* (1915), *Chimera* (oak, 1915), *The Sorceress* (maple, 1916), *Adam and Eve* (old oak, 1920) and *Plato* (1920). The first, three-part *Endless Column*—old oak, 252 centimeters high, on a stone base—dates from 1918; the spacing of its rhomboidal shapes may have been inspired by the fragment of African painting Modigliani made Dr Alexandre pose in front of for his portrait of 1911-12.

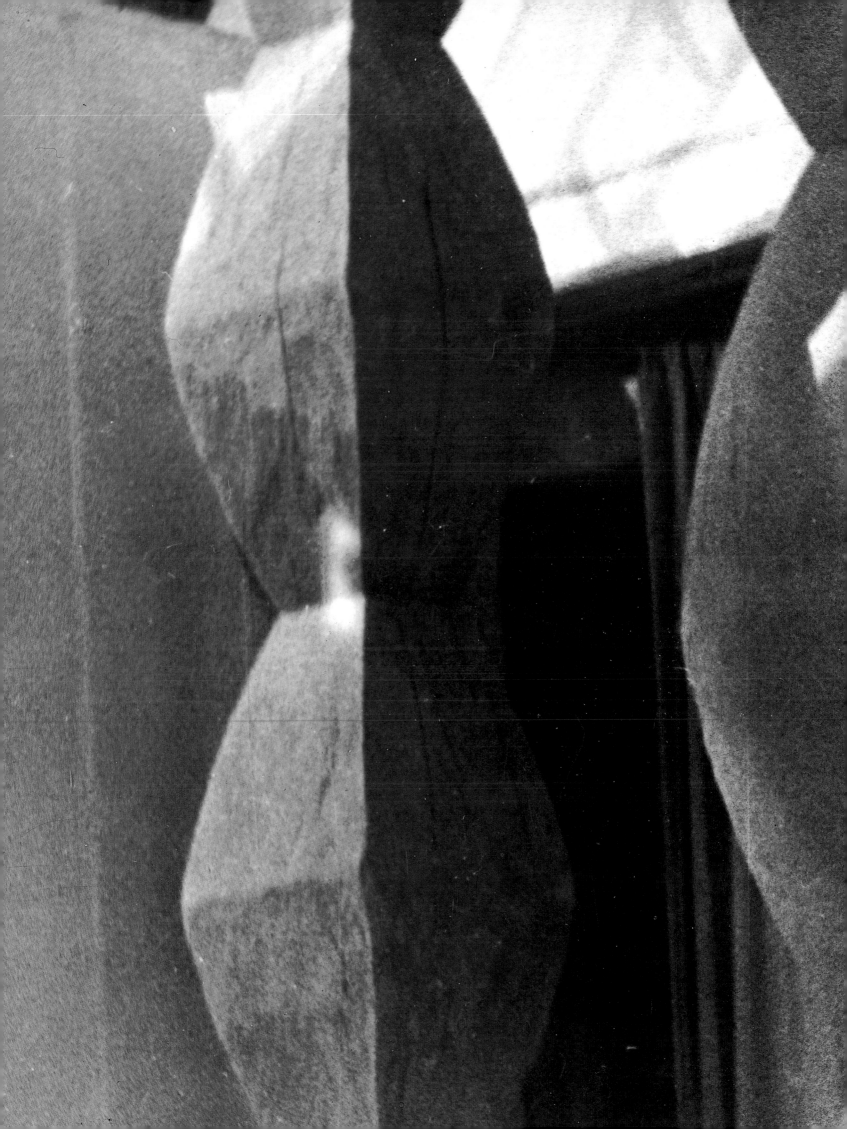

United States, where his principal admirers were to be found, but Brancusi refused.

It was during this period that he created a work at the opposite extreme from his tribally inspired pieces. Made of marble and set on a stone base, *The Newborn*[31] returns to the theme of the ovoid head of a child, of *Sleeping Muse* and *Prometheus*, that elemental, eternal shape that speaks of the beginning and the end of the world. The features are barely suggested and the slightly parted lips will not open further until *The First Cry*[32] in polished bronze, whose tension is reminiscent of that of the head of *The First Step*.

The "idea of a pure form", as Ezra Pound described it, would dog Brancusi all his life. In his major article about Brancusi in the *Little Review* in 1921, Pound remarked that his friend, "when he expresses himself clearly", asserts that art is not "a hysterical fit" and that "beauty has nothing to do with grimaces and chance movements".

He goes on to add that "One reaches a near-mathematical exactness of proportions by starting with an ideal of form, though not by using mathematics…" First and foremost, Pound summed up: "He is a man who loves perfection."

Princess X
1909/1916
Photo Constantin Brancusi
MNAM-Centre G. Pompidou, Paris

Woman Looking Into a Mirror
1909
Silver gelatin print
Photo Constantin Brancusi
MNAM-Centre G. Pompidou, Paris

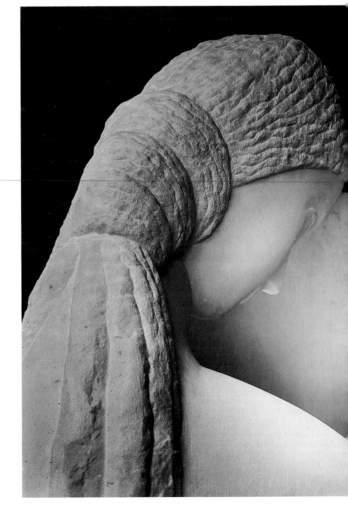

Previous pages:
Two views of the studio
1920
Silver gelatin prints
Photo Constantin Brancusi
MNAM-Centre G. Pompidou, Paris

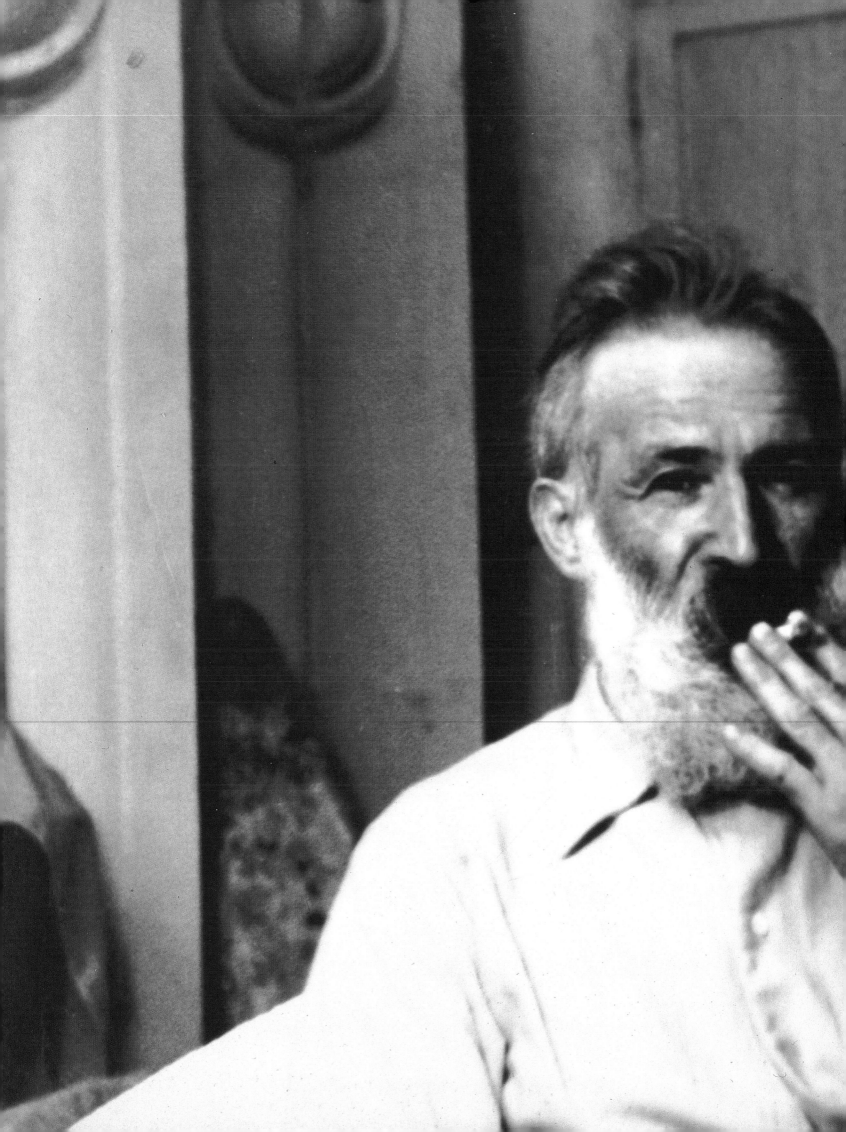

4

1919-1937
Soaring

BIRDS AND A BESTIARY

**View of the studio
with marble bird**
c. 1922/1923
Silver gelatin print
Photo Constantin Brancusi
MNAM-Centre G. Pompidou, Paris

**Self-portrait
in the studio**
1933/1934
Silver gelatin print
Photo Constantin Brancusi
MNAM-Centre G. Pompidou, Paris

n 1919 *Golden Bird* in polished bronze[33] and *Yellow Bird* in yellow marble[34], both born of *Maiastra* and both acquired by John Quinn, began their soaring flight through space and Brancusi's oeuvre, which would ultimately include some thirty variants on the theme. "I'm not sculpting birds," he used to say, "but flight." In these serene, smoothly minimalist forms, with their energy concentrated in their contours, interiority and mass seem secondary considerations beside a symbol so closely akin to the propeller that had fascinated the sculptor at the Air Show years before. Brancusi endlessly photographed his birds, with their different materials and different bases, altering their position in relation to other works in the studio and scrutinizing their luster and cast shadows in his search for multiple visions of a presence meant for air and light. These are works of which the essence transcends their materials even as they assert their physicality and weight in the radiance of the sun.

In 1917 Brancusi suggested a new concept to Quinn, that of the "mobile group", a cluster of initially autonomous works determined by the relationships or the intervening spaces created by their proximity. He organized his shapes according to similarity, setting or contrast, first applying the notion to his studio, where he distinguished between wood, marble and stone, plaster and metal, roughness and smoothness, curves and straight lines, solid objects and empty space,

the small and the monumental, verticality and horizontality—all the components of a living, richly complex creative space.

At the same period his personal image was taking shape, that of the man in white in his white retreat—even Polaire, his dog, was white—splitting oak with an ax, piling stones, polishing marble and metal, and assembling cubes, cylinders and spheres. In the evenings he read Milarepa and the Greek philosophers, unless he was with his friends in the Montparnasse bars, still open in spite of the war. Sometimes he may have received a lady visitor.

On 10 November 1917, Rodin died in Meudon. The previous *May Parade*, the ballet by Cocteau, Picasso and Satie, had been presented at the Châtelet and scandalized all Paris. In Leyden, Mondrian and Van Doesburg, whom Brancusi had known well in Paris, were creating De Stijl, "the style", in all its rigorous austerity. Malevich, inventor and prophet of Suprematism, was pursuing his ideological quest and in 1915 showed his famous *Black Square* in Saint Petersburg. Suprematism, he declared, was the painting of "pure sensation", the "sentiment of the absence of the object". In 1917 he began working on his ideal architecture projects and as his reputation grew he discovered his first disciples in Moscow. The October Revolution brought drastic change to the relationship between art and the public, driving the abstract painter Kandinsky to take refuge in the civil service and teaching.

In June 1917 an accident at a woman friend's house in Chausse, in the south of France, left Brancusi immobilized for several months. Unable to work, he was told by his regular correspondent John Quinn that the latter was finding his prices "a little too high" and would have to cut back on his purchases. Once back on his feet, Brancusi finished the

Lizica Codreanu wearing the stage costume designed for her by Brancusi for Erik Satie's *Gymnopédies*
1922
Photo Constantin Brancusi

View of the studio with two Birds in Space and Princess X
c. 1924
Silver gelatin print
Photo Constantin Brancusi
MNAM-Centre G. Pompidou, Paris

● **Bird in Space**
1927
Silver gelatin print
Photo Constantin Brancusi
MNAM-Centre G. Pompidou, Paris

● **Bird in Space**
1931/1936
Silver gelatin print
Photo Constantin Brancusi
MNAM-Centre G. Pompidou, Paris

Previous pages:
Birds in Space
● **and Endless Column**

● **Self-portrait**
Undated
Silver gelatin print
Photo Constantin Brancusi
MNAM-Centre G. Pompidou, Paris

In 1921 Ezra Pound introduced Brancusi to Eileen Lane, a beautiful American of Irish extraction and a friend of Erik Satie: it was love at first sight for both. Many years later, the elderly woman whose youthful beauty Brancusi had caught in a photographic portrait, still recalled his personal magnetism; despite her frequent stays in the United States, their affair lasted until the outbreak of war in 1939 and she is doubtless the subject of the gouache portraits and of several drawings. He took her to Romania with him in 1924 and to avoid any indelicate curiosity or sarcastic comments from his friends and family in Hobitza introduced her as his daughter. An onyx head, now housed in the Brancusi studio at the Musée National d'Art Moderne in Paris, bears her name.

In 1924 a young dancer Brancusi would describe as his fiancée entered his life and remained just long enough to vanish again into the shadows and leave behind a memory of long blond hair and a few now yellowing photographs. What more is known of Marthe, Brancusi's secretary and later companion, whom Duchamp invited, "if it sounds like fun", to his wedding at the Temple de l'Etoile on 8 June 1927?

The alabaster *White Negress*[37] of 1923 is far from a return to the African influence, but rather a recollection, stripped of all non-essentials, of an encounter Brancusi transformed into a mythic vision. As for a number of other works of this period, he accords enormous importance to the base, here a cross-shaped piece of stone that is an integral part of the work and the source of its monumental character. The base is neither a support nor a foil, but the work itself in its ascension from the ground to its apex. At the Brummer Gallery in 1926 Brancusi included several bases on their own, presenting them as plastic elements in their own right.

● **Torso of a Young Man**
1924
Polished bronze
45.5x27.5x17.5 cm
Hirshhorn Museum and Sculpture
Garden, Washington
Gift of Joseph H. Hirshhorn, 1966

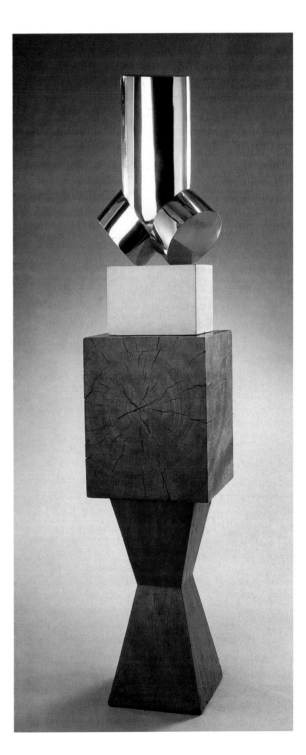

● **Torso of a Girl III**
1925
Onyx
26.7x21.7x16.3 cm
Two-part base: stone and oak
Height: 102 cm
MNAM-Centre G. Pompidou, Paris

PAUL MORAND: BRANCUSI:
"A SCULPTOR OF THE PEOPLE"

On 28 July 1924, John Quinn died of cancer aged fifty-four, leaving an estate that included thirty-three Brancusi sculptures and a drawing. Roché had long known how ill Quinn was and had already devised a plan that would avoid dispersal of the works at a time when the art market was at a very low ebb: he suggested to Duchamp that, with Brancusi's consent, they jointly buy the collection. The deal went through for the reasonable sum of 8,500 dollars and as the opportunity arose they sold Quinn's Brancusis to collectors and museums. With the sculptor's reputation growing steadily in the United States, prices for the works followed suit, especially after exhibitions at the Wildenstein Galleries and the gallery of major collector Joseph Brummer. The Brummer exhibition took place in November-December 1926, organized by Duchamp and with a catalogue prefaced by Paul Morand. The latter's essay presented Brancusi as the anti-Rodin, "a modern man, a sculptor of the people"; it also contributed to the legend of the Romanian peasant with the "long unkempt beard" and "eyes full of Latin cunning and Slav mysticism", a "born craftsman" who works wearing "ill-fitting garments over the body of a workman, a stonecutter, a lumberjack" in a studio that is "a veritable quarry". Morand added, "Perhaps a young, healthy country like the United States is the most suitable home for his work."

BIG COCKS

The geometrical forms of the *Torso of a Young Man*[38], created in 1917-22 by carving a maple trunk at the point where it forked, and of its less schematic successor in walnut, are counterpoised by the smooth curve of the 1920 white marble *Leda*[39], originally set on a double stone base, and by a later polished bronze version, set on a reflective, revolving polished steel disk and now housed in the Musée National d'Art Moderne

View of the studio:
Big Cocks
c. 1940/1945
Silver gelatin print
Photo Constantin Brancusi
MNAM-Centre G. Pompidou, Paris

Blond Negress

c. 1926

Silver gelatin print

Photo Constantin Brancusi

MNAM-Centre G. Pompidou, Paris

Beginning of the world

1920

Silver gelatin print

Photo Constantin Brancusi

MNAM-Centre G. Pompidou, Paris

chignon, that he would finally offer to Teeny Duchamp when she became Marcel's wife in 1954?

Together with Roché, Duchamp—creator of *The Bride Stripped Bare by her Bachelors, Even (The Large Glass)*—became Brancusi's American representative and in November 1934 he organized the sculptor's largest exhibition to date, at the Brummer Gallery. The fifty-seven works on show were enthusiastically received and five were sold for a total of $65,173, an impressive figure for the time. Under the heading "Famous French artist, who has brought Brancusi exhibit to Brummer Gallery, comments wittily on art", *Art News* included an interview with Duchamp, a remarkable tribute to Brancusi and the only one he ever published.

THREE BIRDS MOVE INTO INDORE

Roché—collector, broker, exhibition organizer, specialist in serendipitous encounters, respected in art circles from Paris to New York and Chicago, from London to San Francisco—was as much Duchamp and Brancusi's friend as their business associate. In 1926 he had made the acquaintance of Yeshwant Holkar, the young Maharajah of Indore and a passionate lover of modern art, to whom he sold the polished bronze *Bird in Space*.

Was it Roché or Brancusi who came up with the suggestion that the Maharajah build the temple that had long been the sculptor's dream? Sounding out his friend Quinn, Roché had already, in a letter of 29 March 1922, mentioned that "Brancusi would like to build a temple, something not especially large…" A temple for an American lawyer was a little out of the ordinary, but a Maharajah was something else again! In May 1936 Holkar acquired the remaining two *Birds in Space*, one in black marble, the other in white, and the idea of bringing the three together in a semi-sacred, semi-secular setting began to take

The Maharajah of Indore
Yeshwart Rao Holkar Bahadur
1907/1961

Birds in Space
1931/1936

Left:
Marble
Height: 17.1 cm
Circumference: 44 cm
Stone base
Total height: 184 cm
Australian National Gallery, Canberra

Right:
Black marble
Height: 18.1 cm
Circumference: 47.8 cm
Marble base
Total height: 193.3 cm
Australian National Gallery, Canberra

5

1938-1957
Apotheosis

TIRGU-JIU

The Endless Column
at Tirgu-Jiu
1937/1938
Silver gelatin print
Photo Constantin Brancusi
MNAM-Centre G. Pompidou, Paris

Trial assembly
of the Endless Column
in the Petrosani workshop
1937/1938

Romanian by birth, but living and working in Paris while depending on American art circles for recognition, Brancusi never lost touch with his homeland, visiting often and remaining in contact with its diplomats, poets, artists and officials. In 1931 the authorities in Ploesti, capital of the Prahova district and a major cultural center, had approached him regarding a monument to the famous playwright Ion Luca Caragiali. Brancusi proposed his *Endless Column* and even though the project came to nothing, the Romanian government awarded him the Cultural Order of Merit.

Some years later the National Women's League of Gorj, in Romania, asked Brancusi to create a memorial to those who had fallen in the Great War. President of the League was the young abstract painter Aretia Tatarascu, who had restarted the Oltenia tapestry workshops, where she then worked. Brancusi expressed willingness and discussions began, but he did not want to settle for a single monument: his plan was for an architectural ensemble with the *Endless Column* as its focal point. It would be erected at Tirgu-Jiu in the Jiu Valley, some twenty kilometers from Hobitza, the village of his birth.

The central Street of Heroes was to be marked out with the monument's different components. The site Brancusi had chosen was an enormous empty space in a wooded park on the banks of the Jiu, with houses and streets partially visible through a line of trees. Like Dubuffet, he wan-

Setting up the Endless
Column at Tirgu-Jiu
1937
Silver gelatin print

Endless Column
1937/1938
Silver gelatin print
Photo Constantin Brancusi
MNAM-Centre G. Pompidou, Paris

ted his monumental works to be part of everyday life, with people coming and going or stopping to take a break. He was to be luckier than Dubuffet, whose wishes for *Hourloupe* were totally disregarded. In 1937-38, apart from the National Women's League of Gorj and the gifted artist Aretia Tatarascu—whose husband, as Romania's Prime Minister, had a certain clout—what institution or government would have given an abstract sculptor the green light for something as large-scale as Tirgu-Jiu practically in the center of town? Brancusi was in fact doubly lucky as the League had originally intended to entrust the memorial to the young woman sculptor Militza Patrasco, a great admirer of his work who stood down in his favor.

The Tirgu-Jiu monument comprises three main parts: the *Endless Column*, based on the wood version previously standing in the Steichens' garden in Voulangis, is a series of stacked cast iron rhomboids 29.3-meter high, threaded over an internal steel column and sprayed with molten brass. It weighs some twenty-nine tons. The round *Table of Silence*, made of Bampotoc limestone quarried near Simeria, and surrounded by stools of Cimpulung stone, is a place of meditation, but also a symbol of the family: Brancusi's compatriots saw in it an allusion to the round table of the peasant households of his native region, and the same kind of table and seats were to be found in his Paris studio.

A section of the Endless
Column, before being set up
August 1937
Tirgu-Jiu

View of the studio
1930/1933
Silver gelatin print
Photo Constantin Brancusi
MNAM-Centre G. Pompidou, Paris

Bordered by square stone seats, the walk leading from the *Table of Silence* to the *Gate of the Kiss* is called the Avenue of the Chairs. Sitting here, the visitor can meditate on the massive, strictly geometrical Bampotoc stone gate, its crosspiece resting on twin pillars each comprising two vertical blocks. Almost 5-meter high, 6.6-meter wide and surrounded by trees, it would seem to represent a place of transition between nature and life and the world of the spirit. Its lightly incised decoration refers to the folkdance known as the *hora*, danced in a ring and closing with a kiss. The main figures of the dance are described in stylized patterns that encircle the monument in a continuous movement Oscar Han likened to "the rhythmic stamping of the foresters' *hora* in the Hunedoara region". The surfaces of the pillars also bear the symbol of the kiss, the finale of the *hora*.

The avenue linking the *Gate* and the *Column* is broken by an immense traffic circle on which rises the Church of Saint Peter and Saint Paul; the building clashes badly with the overall plan, but Brancusi, although far from happy, had to put up with it. The grand opening of the Tirgu-Jiu monument took place on 27 October 1938 in the presence of its creator and local government officials. Mass was celebrated and the *Endless Column* was sprinkled with holy water by a bevy of ecclesiastics.

The French press did not mention the event at the time. Nor had Brancusi attended the major "Art Indépendant" exhibition held in the

Petit Palais as part of the 1937 World Fair; an *Endless Column* had been planned for the garden of the Romanian pavilion, but ultimately he was represented only indoors, by a single *Little Bird* in marble.

His work had still to find a place in the collection of the Musée National d'Art Moderne in Paris' Palais de Tokyo and it was not until 1946 that the French State finally purchased *Sleeping Muse*, *The Cock* and *The Seal*.

A NEW *BIRD* AND VARIANTS ON *THE KISS*

The many photographs Brancusi took in his studios allow us to follow the development of his oeuvre and his creation of shifting relationships both between individual sculptures and between his work and its setting. Here we see polished bronze alongside white and colored marble, stone side by side with wood, and groupings dominated by the various *Endless Columns*. Sometimes he himself posed among his sculptures, clad in his usual work outfit.

Endless Column

1937/1938
Silver gelatin print

Photo Constantin Brancusi

MNAM-Centre G. Pompidou, Paris

The enormous photographic collection now held by the Centre Pompidou in Paris includes some five hundred original negatives and twelve hundred and fifty prints. In the small laboratory he set up, Brancusi produced two or more prints from each negative, varying the size and framing. For him these photos were a precious aspect of his work, while for the viewer, transported into the sculptor's studio, they now represent a voyage to the heart of his oeuvre and his vision.

With Tirgu-Jiu completed and Indore regretfully abandoned, Brancusi was contacted by the director of the Romanian pavilion at the 1939 New York World Fair. The idea was to exhibit his work in a purpose-built room, but nothing came of it. In between he had spent the period August 1938-May 1939 he remained in the United States, meeting art dealers and collectors but continued to be ignored by their French counterparts. He also contributed to exhibitions in Amsterdam, London, New York and Chicago. In Paris Yvonne Zervos showed him at the Galerie Mai, accompanied with works by Arp, Gonzalez, Klee and Henri Laurens.

Roché was still visiting the studio regularly, in spite of Brancusi's complaints at his separation of the three Indore *Birds;* Duchamp, on the other hand, was spending most of his time in the United States and the two saw each other less. Now something of a recluse, Brancusi was working less and slowly polishing earlier pieces. The coming of the war cut him off from his American contacts and left him at something of a loss. In 1941 he rented a fifth adjoining studio where he produced a new *Bird in Space* of polished bronze, setting it on a stone base. Another new creation was a yellow stone *Kiss,* the heads elongated and the embrace taking place at the mid-point of the sculpture. *Boundary Marker;* a further variant on the same work, comprises three stacked sections whose lightly incised surfaces are reminiscent of the *Gate* at Tirgu-Jiu. This same period—1941-43—saw a second *Seal* in veined gray

The Kiss
1907
Stone
28x26x21.5 cm
Hamburg Kunsthalle, Hamburg

Bird in Space
1930
Silver gelatin print
Photo Constantin Brancusi
MNAM-Centre G. Pompidou, Paris

marble, set on two stone table-tops of which the upper one was turned by a motor. These last three works can now be seen in Brancusi's reconstructed studio in Paris.

In New York in February 1942 the Buchholz Gallery presented its "From Rodin to Brancusi" exhibition, a brief historical survey of contemporary sculpture.

PEGGY GUGGENHEIM REMEMBERS...

In the vast drawing room of her Palazzo Venier dei Leoni home on the Grand Canal in Venice, surrounded by Italian surrealist paintings and African sculptures, Peggy Guggenheim reminisces about Brancusi, to whom she had been introduced by Marcel Duchamp. In the studio on Impasse Ronsin, she recalls, the white sculptures covered in dust immediately gave her the feeling of being in a cemetery. Yet in her memoirs, *Out of this Century: Confessions of an art addict* she makes no secret of the fascination the sculptor held for her: "Brancusi was a marvelous little man with a beard and dark, piercing eyes, a mix of crafty peasant and genius…He always did his best to make you happy when you were with him. Unfortunately he became very possessive and wanted me there all the time. He called me "Pegitza"…"

Gradually, the calm of Venice and of a later time she confides more. Relations between herself and Brancusi could have taken quite a different turn, she admits, if she had gone traveling with him as he had asked her to, but his possessiveness frightened her. She was well aware—and he would not have been displeased by this—of his penchant for amatory conquests, but found his persecution mania ominous: "He was convinced he was being spied on." And in spite of all his declarations of love, "He never gave me a single present." For his part, he feared a relationship would let her start filching his work.

It transpires that, Peggy Guggenheim was very keen to acquire a number of works for her collection, but Brancusi drove a hard bargain. Her first acquisition came in 1940 with the sale of the couturier Paul Poiret's estate: a 1912 polished bronze *Maiastra* on a trapezoidal stone base, for which she paid $1,000. The same year she managed to

The Seal II
1943
Blue-gray marble
110.5x121.5x34 cm
MNAM-Centre G. Pompidou, Paris

Alfred Courmes
Portrait of Peggy Guggenheim
August 1926
Oil on canvas
31.5x23 cm
Musée de La Coopération
Franco-Américaine, Blérancourt,
on loan from the Musée d'Orsay

wrench from the sculptor a polished bronze *Bird in Space* dating from 1930, but this time the exercise cost her $4,000. Several months later, Peggy Guggenheim recounts, when the Germans were marching on Paris and she had to leave, Brancusi was in tears; but she never knew if the source of his grief was the separation from her or from his favorite work.

In 1940-41, however, a new *Bird in Space*—at 194 centimeters the largest of them all—emerged from the sculptor's magical hands to be set on a triple stone base. Once polished, he set it up in his studio against a backdrop of Pompeian red, to gleam majestically in the light pouring in through the glass.

The end of the war saw visitors returning to the studio and scattered articles beginning to appear proclaiming the solitary Brancusi as one of the great sculptors of the century. At last, thanks to Jean Cassou, the French State had bought three of his works, and exhibi-

The Blond Negress
The Steichen column
1926
Silver gelatin print
MNAM-Centre G. Pompidou, Paris

Peggy Guggenheim
in her palace in Venice
c. 1960

tions, many of them tributes, were being mounted all over the world. Helped by his neighbor and compatriot Istrati, he set about the enduring obsession of his last years, the five-meter *Cock* now to be seen in the reconstructed studio. Although he kept on working, he seemed indifferent to everything except the preservation of his œuvre after his death.

In the 1950s Peggy Guggenheim came back to Paris and visited Brancusi in Impasse Ronsin with Nellie Van Doesburg, widow of the painter who, with Mondrian and another friend, had founded "De Stijl". They were received with all the affability he usually showed to lady visitors, Brancusi asking about *Maiastra* and *Bird in Space,* which she had lent to the Venice Biennale in 1947. He mentioned the belated interest of the State, but his voice was tinged with sadness, as if he were on the verge of being robbed of what was rightfully his. Fresh threats were hanging over his studios and he admitted to thinking about the United States as an alternative to losing everything. If they were married, Peggy interjected laughingly, there would be no problem.

Brancusi served them drinks and little dishes of his own concoction, angrily brushing aside their attempts to help, before taking them on a tour of the studio, removing the slip covers from his sculptures, turning *Leda* on its base, firing off comments on his reading—mostly Milarepa—and showing his disappointment at their ignorance of his favorite Tibetan sage. With the arrival of his assistants and watchdogs the Istratis, doubtless aware of his earlier relationship with Peggy Guggenheim and convinced she was there to fleece him, the hitherto friendly atmosphere became tinged with suspicion. Under their vigilant eye an increasingly edgy Peggy talked about her Foundation in the palace in Venice, Brancusi asked if his works would be shown to their best advantage there, and with the situation becoming increasingly formal and stilted the visitors took their leave. This was Peggy's last visit to her aging admirer.

IONESCO'S *THE CHAIRS* IN BRANCUSI'S STUDIO

No longer working at his sculpture, Brancusi prowled his studios, took naps and spent hours on his doorstep watching the occasional passers-by, but remained taciturn with his neighbors. Sometimes he ventured out for a stroll in what was still pretty much a small town, a familiar figure to the local storekeepers with his white fur bonnet, white tunic and white stick, his trousers concertinaed over his clogs and a loose black sweater added when it turned cold.

In spite of his low opinion of the theatre, he wanted to see a playwright in the flesh and invited Ionesco, a fellow Romanian and a friend of Istrati and Dumitresco. Launching into a series of incomprehensible and frequently aggressive ramblings, he eventually realized that Ionesco was not particularly interested and changed tack, reminiscing about his life. Later, one New Year's Eve in his declining years, a group of actors turned up at the studio and played Ionesco's *The Chairs;* extremely touched, Brancusi prepared two legs of lamb, one in the oven and the other in his forge, and the meal was generously washed down with champagne. As was his habit, Brancusi retired early[45].

Ionesco, at once startled and awed by the old artist's talk and behavior, would subsequently speak of the inspiring experience of having met a great actor.

Brancusi had not seen Duchamp for a long time, but received a letter from him in 1953 informing him that J. J. Sweeney, the new director of the Solomon Guggenheim Museum, was hoping to organize a retrospective and that he, Duchamp (who doubtless still had some of his

Three Penguins
1911/1912
Marble
56.5x52.8x34.3 cm
Philadelphia Museum of Art
The Louise and Walter Arensberg Collection

Beginning of the World
1924
Polished bronze
17.8x28.5x17.6 cm
Two-part base:
polished steel and wood
Height: 75 cm
MNAM-Centre G. Pompidou, Paris

Quinn estate pieces to sell) would be in charge. With requests being made on all sides, Brancusi did not follow up the offer, but the retrospective—fifty-nine sculptures together with ten drawings and gouaches—took place two years later. It then traveled to the Philadelphia Museum.

Some years earlier the old man had met François Stahly, a young sculptor and a friend of Roché. They had spoken of their mutual interest in oriental philosophy and beliefs and Brancusi was impressed by the other's knowledgeability. He agreed to let Stahly polish—under his supervision, of course—a *Bird* and a *Cock* on a grand scale to be made for sites in New York and Chicago; however the relationship was a difficult one and Brancusi abruptly terminated the arrangement. Stahly, in spite of his admiration for the older man, found him authoritarian and resentful of any contradiction: "His conversation, he related, was based on a weird, constantly reinvented mythology with himself as the magus, the seer in contact with extra-terrestrials…Lots of apparently influential figures visited the studio, most of them English-speakers." Some of these visitors almost seemed to consider the sculptor a kind of guru.

A series of accidents late in 1954 saw Brancusi confined to his bed for several months. Duchamp and Roché came to visit for his birthday on 21 February 1955: the New York and Philadelphia retrospectives had been enormously successful and the press had been full of praise.

● **Leda**
1925/1926
Silver gelatin print
Photo Constantin Brancusi
MNAM-Centre G. Pompidou, Paris

A naturalized French citizen since 1 May 1952, Brancusi now decided to bequeath his remaining oeuvre to the nation: it comprised one hundred and fifty-eight sculptures (not counting their bases) which he regarded as inseparable from the studio itself, together with the other contents of the studio: plaster originals, handmade furniture and tools, and his library and photographic files. He stipulated that the studio should be re-created as it was on Impasse Ronsin. The details of this truly remarkable donation were included in his will dated 12 April 1956, which also named the Istratis as sole legatees.

NOSTALGIA IN THE STUDIO

One final muse was to slip into his studio, a discreet presence amid the stone and marble: Valentine Hugo, former friend of the Surrealists and of André Breton in particular. She had also known Radiguet, and he had been the first to speak to her, "fervently", of this "near-legendary figure whom I imagined as mysterious, diffident, reclusive, locked away with his work in a studio surrounded by an enchanted garden." The enchantment had gone, however, leaving only the ramshackle studios that the Social Welfare Department was longing to get its hands on—and where, on the door of number 7, Valentine Hugo saw the name "Brancusi" written in chalk[46].

Entering, she saw the sculptor "dressed in white working clothes with that sundrenched, ivory tinge you get on rough, handwoven fabric…" Brancusi introduced himself. "I didn't dare," she stammered, "all this time, and now here I am…" He sat her beside him at a kind of stone table and there before her in the silence of the studio were the *Cocks*, the *Endless Columns*, the *Birds*, *Caryatid*, *Fish* and not least, *King of Kings*. Clearly in pain from his rheumatism, the sculptor—as attentive as ever to the opposite sex—gave her a guided tour of the other studios, where she discovered earlier pieces: a "diaphanous" *Sleeping Muse*,

View of the studio
Cat-Caryatid
1924
Silver gelatin print
Photo Constantin Brancusi
MNAM-Centre G. Pompidou, Paris

and then *Leda*, "unbound, gleaming, slowly turning and turning on its mirror of frozen metal…and the great marble turtle, ready to take flight and bear away its dome."

They began to speak of the past, of absent friends, and little by little the spell overtook her. "It seemed to me," she later said, "that I could no longer live without the atmosphere of calmness, courage and wisdom surrounding this singular man, descendant of a proud line…" She returned several times to this oasis of peace, a vestige of another time; and the lone wolf revealed an unsuspected mildness with a woman once so famous and so desired, who during her life had known everyone worth knowing. In the white-bearded hermit, obsessed with the survival of his studios and what they contained, she discovered "a tranquil nobility, an assurance and joie de vivre, an endlessly renewed will to keep going…"

It was suggested at one point that the Impasse Ronsin studios should be transferred to Meudon, to the vast premises used by Rodin to produce an oeuvre diametrically opposed to Brancusi's, but the project was abandoned. When Roché visited his friend early in 1957 he found him very frail and "endlessly humming the same tunes". Brancusi died on 15 March, aged eighty.

Arp had once written: "Day was falling, but the space about a bird, lost in dreams of feathered lightning, failed to see that the bird had flown, swooping down the path to the studio of the endless column.

Cock-a-doodle-doo sang the cock, each sound making a zig then a zag down its throat Brancusi's cock is saw-toothed with joy.

Sawing the day of the tree of light."

The funeral service was held at the Romanian church on Rue Jean-de-Beauvais, where Brancusi had once served as deacon. At the burial in the Montparnasse cemetery, Man Ray was staggered to see a massive bouquet brought by a delegation from the Romanian embassy, representing a communist government that had come within an ace of demolishing Tirgu-Jiu. Some of those present were very vocal in their disapproval. "It was really very depressing," Man Ray said later. "I made a resolution never to go to a burial again."

Man Ray
Portrait of Valentine Hugo
1935

Big Cocks in the reconstructed Brancusi studio

MNAM-Centre G. Pompidou, Paris

A PLACE OF MAGIC LOST

The initial reconstruction of the studio in the Musée d'Art Moderne at the Palais de Tokyo—intended as a work of art in its own right, complete with furniture, tools, everyday objects, glass walls and marble dust, but suffering from a ceiling that was too low—was not a success. When the Museum was transferred to the Centre Pompidou, the ugly building erected on the square bore little resemblance to the Impasse Ronsin original, now reclaimed by the Social Welfare Department and razed to make way for the Necker Hospital.

In 1996 Renzo Piano, one of the designers of the Centre Pompidou, was asked to replace this haphazard reconstruction with a copy, based on the old plans, of what was Brancusi's lair for almost half a century. Yet the result is a curiously clinical interior running directly counter to the spirit and layout of the original: there is no public access to the works, which are presented behind plate glass windows—as if in a department store—and can only be viewed from the surrounding corridor. To make matters worse, the glass picks up the reflections of the Centre and the neighboring buildings. The place of magic has gone and the intimacy of the temple to hard work has given way to another frigid museum with everything labeled and everything in its place in a context of inflexible orderliness. The visitor's perception of the work is totally changed. "My life has been a succession of miracles," Brancusi used to say. But there were none after his death.

Man Ray
Portrait of Brancusi
holding his dog Polaire
1930

French State, on condition that his studio be rebuilt, "preferably in the Musée d'Art Moderne". From November 1956 to January 1957, a major exhibition at the Metropolitan Museum in New York.

1957. In February, an exhibition in homage to Brancusi at the People's Museum of Art in Bucharest. Brancusi dies on 16 March. After the funeral on the 19th at the Romanian Orthodox Church in the Rue Jean-de-Beauvais, where he had once been deacon, he is buried in the Montparnasse cemetery, not far from *The Kiss*. Tributes follow at the Salon de Mai and the Salon de la Jeune Sculpture in June.

The above chronology has been drawn from *Brancusi* by Pontus Hulten, Alexandre Istrati and Natalia Dumitresco; *Brancusi* by Radu Varia; *Constantin Brancusi* by Carola Giedion-Welcker, *Sur les pas de Brancusi* by Serge Fauchereau, *Out of this Century: Confessions of an art addict* by Peggy Guggenheim, Scarlett and Philippe Reliquet, *Henri-Pierre Roché, l'enchanteur collectionneur*, and publications and archival material from the Centre Georges Pompidou, Paris.

1876. Second "Impressionist" exhibition. Manet illustrates Mallarmé's *Afternoon of a Faun*. Renoir: *At the Moulin de la Galette*.
1880. Rodin: *The Thinker*
1881. Manet: *A Bar at the Folies-Bergères*. Degas: *Little Fourteen-year-old Dancer*. Birth of Picasso.
1883. The painter Caillebotte donates his collection to the French State. Whistler shows *Portrait of the Painter's Mother*. Huysmans publishes *L'Art Moderne*. Monet moves to Giverny. Cézanne is painting at L'Estaque.
1884. First Salon des Indépendants. Death of Manet.
1885. Seurat: *Sunday Afternoon on the Island of La Grande Jatte*.
1888-89. Ensor paints his *Entry of Christ into Brussels*. The "Nabis" group is formed. Gauguin in Brittany, then in Arles with Van Gogh.
1890. Rodin-Monet exhibition at the Galerie Georges Petit. Death of Van Gogh.
1895. Rodin: *The Burghers of Calais*.
1898. Rodin shows *Balzac* at the Salon de la Société Nationale des Beaux-Arts. Gauguin in Tahiti.
1899. Degas: *Blue Dancers*.
1900. Paris World's Fair. Picasso's first trip to Paris. Monet: *Waterlilies*.
1903. Death of Gauguin. Auguste Perret: world's first reinforced concrete building.
1904. Matisse: *Luxe, Calme et Volupté*. Cézanne begins his paintings of *Mont Sainte-Victoire*. Picasso moves into the Bateau-Lavoir in Paris.
1905. The Fauves at the Salon d'Automne
1906. Death of Cézanne. Rodin's *Thinker* erected in front of the Pantheon.
1907. Picasso: *Les Demoiselles d'Avignon*. Beginnings of Cubism. Degas: pastels of dancers. The Douanier Rousseau at the Salon d'Automne.
1908. Braque painting at L'Estaque. Rodin moves into the Hôtel Biron (now the Musée Rodin).

1909. Manet's *Olympia* in the Louvre. First Futurist manifesto.
1910. Kandinsky paints the first abstract watercolor. Matisse: *Dance and Music*.
1911. Kandinsky publishes *Concerning the Spiritual in Art*.
1912. Braque's first papier collé pieces. Orphism.

NOTES

1. Radu Varia, Brancusi, Paris, 1989.
2. The low-relief of Surgeon-General Carol Davila is in the Matei Basarab high school in Bucharest; the bust, cast in bronze in 1912, is in the military hospital there. The bust of Ion Georgescu-Gorjan is in the Bucharest museum.
3. Pontus Hulten, Alexandre Istrati, Natalia Dumitresco, *Brancusi*, Abrams, New York, 1987
4. Most of the original plasters have been lost, but bronzes are to be found in the Museum of Fine Arts in Bucharest and in private collections in Bucharest, New York and Paris.
5. The local roots of Brancusi's work are remarkably illustrated in Serge Fauchereau, *Sur les pas de Brancusi*, Paris, 1995.
6. It has been replaced in Buzau cemetery by a copy in stone.
7. Craiova Museum
8. Petru Comarnesco, "Universel et national dans l'œuvre de Brancusi", in *Revue roumaine d'histoire de l'art*, no. 1, 1966.
9. Sidney Geist, "Brancusi", in William Rubin (ed.), *Primitivism in 20th Century Art*, New York, 1984
10. This unhappy love affair is related by the Romanian art critic Barbau Brezianu from the account given by Clara Marbais, widow of the involuntary hero in "Le secret du Baiser de Brancusi", in *Revue du Louvre*, 1961, no. 1
11. Museum of Fine Arts, Bucharest
12. Former Apollinaire collection of plasters from Brancusi's studio, Centre Georges Pompidou, Paris
13. Mircea Eliade, June 1967, in Ionel Jianou, *Brancusi*, Paris, 1982
14. Private collection
15. Pontus Hulten, Alexandre Istrati, Natalia Dumitresco, *op. cit.*
16. See Edith Balas, "The Myth of African Negro Art in Brancusi's Sculpture", in *Revue roumaine d'histoire de l'art*, 1977, no. 14; Katherine Janszky Michaelsen, "Brancusi and African Art", in *Art Forum*, November 1971; Sidney Geist, *op. cit.*
17. Brancusi Archives, Musée National d'Art Moderne, Paris
18. The Hirshhorn Museum and Sculpture Garden (Smithsonian Institution), Washington
19. Pontus Hulten, Alexandre Istrati, Natalia Dumitresco, *op. cit.*
20. In 1947 Rousseau's grave was transferred to the cemetery of Bagneux in Laval, where he had been born in 1844

21. MOMA, NY, Katherine S. Dreier donation
22. Athena Tacha Spear, "Les Oiseaux de Brancusi", in *L'Oiseau dans l'espace*, Carnets de l'Atelier Brancusi, Centre Georges Pompidou, Paris
23. Private collection, Bern, Switzerland
24. Philadelphia Museum of Art, Philadelphia, Arensberg donation
25. Annie Cohen-Solal, *Un jour ils auront des peintres*, Paris, Gallimard, 2000
26. Museum of Modern Art, New York. Four copies were cast of this bronze with a patina on the hair: of the three others one is in the Bucharest Museum and a second in the J.B. Speed Museum in Louisville, Kentucky. The whereabouts of the third are unknown. The veined marble *Mademoiselle Pogany II* of 1919 is in the James W. Alsdorf collection in Chicago. A polished bronze dating from 1920 is in the Albright-Knox Gallery in Buffalo, two others are in the Rio de Janeiro Museum and the Katherine Ordway collection in New York. Another polished bronze, from 1925, is in the Morton Gallery, West Palm Beach. A plaster of the same year is in the Brancusi Studio at the Centre Georges Pompidou in Paris.
27. Philadelphia Museum of Art
28. Sidney Geist, *op. cit.*
29. The Solomon Guggenheim Museum, New York
30. Private collection, Paris
31. Philadelphia Museum (Arensberg donation)
32. Lady Nika Hulton collection, London
33. Arts Club of Chicago and Minneapolis Institute of Arts
34. Yale University Art Gallery
35. The Solomon Guggenheim Museum, New York
36. The Museum of Modern Art, New York
37. Philadelphia Museum of Art (Arensberg donation)
38. *Idem*
39. Art Institute of Chicago.
40. Margit Rowell, Brancusi vs. United States: The Historic Trial, 1928, Vilo International, 1999
41. National Gallery of Art, Washington
42. Estate of Mrs Marcel Duchamp
43. The Solomon Guggenheim Museum, New York
44. See Marielle Tabard and Isabelle Monod-Fontaine, *Brancusi Photographer*, Agrinde-Zebriskie, 1977
45. Eugène Ionesco, *Notes and Counter Notes: Writings on the Theater*, Grove Press, 1964
46. Valentine Hugo in *Cahiers d'Art*, 1956

SELECT BIBLIOGRAPHY

- Ionel Jianou, *Constantin Brancusi*, Paris, 1963.
- Carole G.Welcker, *Constantin Brancusi*, Neuchâtel, 1958.
- David Lewis, *Constantin Brancusi*, London, 1974.
- Eric Shanes, *Constantin Brancusi*, New York, 1989.
- Edith Balas, *Brancusi, und Rumanian Folk Traditions*, East European Monographs, 1987
- Mircea Deâc, *Constantin Brancusi*, Bucharest, 1966.
- Sidney Geist, *Brancusi – The Kiss*, New York, 1978.
- Sidney Geist, *Brancusi – A Study of the Sculpture*, Grossman, New York,1968.
- Ionel Jianou, Mircea Eliade, Petru Comarnescu, *Témoignages sur Brancusi*, Paris, 1967.

- Marielle Tabart, Isabelle Monod-Fontaine, *Brancusi photographer*, Agrinde-Zebriskie, 1977.
- Radu Varia, *Brancusi*, New York, 1986
- Barbu Brezianu, *Opera lui Constantin Brancusi in România*, Bucharest, 1974.
- Anna Chave, *Constantin Brancusi – Shifting the Bases of Art*, Yale, 1993.
- Pontus Hulten, Alexandre Istrati, Natalia Dumitresco, *Brancusi*, Abrams, New York, 1987.
- Serge Fauchereau, *Sur les pas de Brancusi*, Paris, Cercle d'art, 1995.
- Margit Rowell, *Brancusi vs. United States: The Historic Trial, 1928*, Vilo International, 1999.
- Marielle Tabart, *Brancusi. L'Inventeur de la sculpture moderne*, Gallimard, Paris, 1995.
- Scarlett et Philipe Reliquet, *Henri-Pierre Roché. L'enchanteur collectionneur*, Ramsay, Paris, 2000.

The collection "Les Carnets de l'Atelier Brancusi", Centre Pompidou, Paris, includes *La Colonne sans fin*, *Léda*, *Le Baiser*, *Princesse X*, *L'Oiseau dans l'espace*, *Le Portrait*. The collection "Regards historiques" offers *Brancusi et Duchamp*.

PHOTOGRAPHIC CREDITS

Printed by EuroGrafica
Vicence - ITALY
May 2002